BOYS OF MY YOUTH

BOYS OF MY YOUTH

Rebecca Okrent

Four Way Books
Tribeca

Please direct all inquiries to:
Editorial Office
Four Way Books
POB 535, Village Station
New York, NY 10014
www.fourwaybooks.com

Library of Congress Cataloging-in-Publication Data

Okrent, Rebecca.
[Poems. Selections]
Boys of my youth / Rebecca Okrent.
pages cm
ISBN 978-1-935536-60-4 (pbk. : alk. paper)
I. Title.
PS3615.K76A6 2016
811'.6--dc23
                    2015006036

This book is manufactured in the United States of America and printed on acid-free paper.

Four Way Books is a not-for-profit literary press. We are grateful for the assistance
we receive from individual donors, public arts agencies, and private foundations.

This publication is made possible with public funds from the New York State Council on the Arts,
a state agency.

[clmp]

We are a proud member of the Community of Literary Magazines and Presses.

Distributed by University Press of New England
One Court Street, Lebanon, NH 03766

For Dan

and

John and Lydia Okrent

my equally affectionate and loving we

CONTENTS

AUBADE

Heard from the rim of dream
the mourning doves' slowed calliope call,
the crows' chortles, the robin's canticle,
and nearer, the ruffle of wings—
all say this is morning.
But listen, hear the silent heat of noon
waiting in the shadows of the pines
and night, too, is circling back,
as if there were no such things as hours
but only tidal time, a day dropped
on the shore and then withdrawn,
and nothing I can sing will make you stay.

TRUE LOVE

My father's whiskered, whiskey cheek
teaches wanting love is not the same
as wanting safety. My children expose
a trove of passionate affection, ravenous
kisses, magic kisses. What I know
is certain as I powder and blanket,
dim lights or draw back blinds:
that the curse of doing harm already
stalks these rooms and waits.
True love is the very opposite of safe.

AUGUST

Rose, bayberry, and chokecherry shed their sun-streaked garments
and leave him naked to the night, tumbling toward sunset, drink in hand.
The day departs. He watches: the sea seethes, flings itself onto the rocks,
pulls him away from himself as it recedes, and leaves him not quite belonging
anywhere. How did he get so far from Ohio? And if he'd stayed?
Numbed, he's full of feeling: *Come to the window. Sweet's the night air.*
So sweet it breaks his heart and leaves him homesick,
nostalgic for a moment that never arrives.
He can't disentangle his life from his ripening fear. Morose,
he's proud and disappointed. Yearning for an absent one
the self he circumscribed? The son difficult to love?
He steadies himself, arrives at the table
where his wife has placed his plate of noodles.

DANSE MACABRE

Daylight is ferocious,
tears at intention
as a lioness her kill,
so by nightfall resolve
is a carcass, again
you wreath remains
in smoke and ashes, bleach
the bones in bourbon
smut your face in entrails
and pronounce the layers of dark
you fall through
beautiful.

IN THE DOCTOR'S OFFICE

She arranges his chairs as if unrolling
an ancient map—*here be dragons.*
Summoned to their places her silent sons,
the obedient ones who might have filled
the house with sound—
they who withheld their enchantments—
now take their seats, offer protection
from the doctor's prognosis: the only one
who's ever been enough for her will die.
Let's not, any one of us, be real.

THE CROW KILLER

Because they ruin the sky,
besiege the branch,
silence songbirds.
My weapon—a slingshot,
its trajectory a transport—
like Thackeray's wit—
for the common rubble:
His Lordship Humblepebble,
Lady Hardberry, good as bullets,
missiles contrived to put an end to them.
They ride on floating corpses
where blind river dolphins rise
through shrouds of watery waste.
Downriver, crocodiles.
They surround this house,
turn my father's eyes to shallows
and put me in a killing mood.
It's envy that torments me I suppose,
I'd rather be a badass crow
than stuck here knowing
what I can't know.

WAS IT DUST I WAS KISSING?

I want my mother to give
my dying father a Hollywood kiss.
She feeds him strawberries and pecks his brow,
refuses to reckon or curb the gross tumor
pressing into our days. Why can't she
wake him up, make him rave
as he wouldn't even before his tongue died in its cave.

We two sisters curl our bodies against his,
but it's his embrace we crave,
never so safe as now our vexing proximity. Our flesh
is stung by the tender wasp. The worm has a shadow
only as it hangs over the mouth of the trout. Waiting.
Point me toward the far shore where he's waving.

She licked his ashes from her fingers and her palms.

MY FATHER'S ISLAND GARDEN

We wanted hedgerows.
He created a hodgepodge,
Emblem of obstinacy and industry,
Recycling sea wrack,
Enclosing his garden with Midwestern
Ingenuity.
Guardian of potatoes and peas,
Never victorious
Over earwigs or weeds,
Rocks he tortured with levers and fire,
Arm-wrestled to make way for this orchard.
Now he's gone and his garden
Tells his story,
Arrayed by his eye,
Ransacked by honeysuckle vines.
My task
Is to restore,
Eulogize,
Scavenge the dead grasses, the rabbit's
Corpse in the Havahart trap,
Lay the waste in a pile, a pyre, set
Aflame with a page from Matthew Arnold.
Say a prayer:
Here lies his labor,
Be it not in vain.
Yet may he remain here,

Nobly flawed.
I am his daughter.
God, if he were still alive
He would have loved
This poem's disguise.

STAR SAPPHIRE

What might it be worth, this memento
of my parents' fifty-year marriage set
in a diamond and sapphire crown, too large,
too gaudy for my taste?
I pass it under the partition
to the jeweler who holds it to the light,
then under the stern eye of his loupe.
(*Do you see it, young man?* The doctor
asks the consumptive as,
floor pulsing, light snapping,
he stares at the fluoroscope image,
into the skeletal chamber of his cousin's
aquatic heart.) The gemstone might have been mined
in Burma or Ceylon.
The jeweler's sad eyes return to me,
pronounce the fraud: *Synthetic. Union
Carbide 1940's. Thirty dollars. Sorry.*
It's not the wad of bills I regret but the story,
the jewel worth risking a life for, hidden in a bodice
during border crossings. I want
the fedora-topped ancestor killed by a trolley in Moscow,
a shard of unyielding amber in his pocket,
not the Huguenot pioneer felled by a tree on the plains,
the ring supposed to have only sentimental value
until hard times force the lone survivor to sell—
worth more than anyone imagined.

BOYS OF MY YOUTH

In the eyes of my dog I was innocent
though I never was chaste.

~

~

There I am in the woods with Timmy.
Slick-skinned as cowslips, we doffed our clothes
to fully feel lush mosses.

Torn lady's slippers mirrored our anatomy.
We shared phylum with skunk cabbage and fern.
Pretend as sprites, supremely unreasoned, swatted
by sunlight into pure being, cupped in swaths of shade.

~

~

(Into the woods he beckoned me,
the man at the picnic with the puppy.

I was clumsy—did he push me?—fell.
He pulled down my pants.
To spank me for crying?
Yes. *Don't be a crybaby!*
Night after night, loitering in the dark, he haunts my bedroom.
His lumber jacket. His palm.)

I have believed the blind can smell my sin.

~

~

In the middle ages of our progress we invented tortures,
drew labyrinthine penitentiaries with sticks in the dirt.

In my dream we were hung naked from pegs in the basement
for feasting on or to be thrown to the unfathomable undertow.

~

~

When Tom, Joe, and David wouldn't let me in their game
I offered my affliction as reward.
"I'll take down my pants." But they'd had enough of that
and had agreed among themselves that girls were nuisances.
I, too, disliked them.

~

~

Brian brought the dairy barn onto the school bus
with his dung-muddied shoes, then lay his head on his desk and
slept. My sympathy was indwelling, oceanic.

~

~

Because the children from the foster home were damaged
those who would have been obliged to love them didn't.
Harelipped John Payne passed notes from his desk to mine:

I love you. Do you love me? Check yes or no.
I penciled in **maybe**.

Dark-eyed Douglas Murdock spun the bottle then
led me by the hand to a darkened room.
First kiss.

His twin Donald died jumping on their bed *just horsing around.*
The special assembly didn't explain it.

~

~

Boys are so casually sacrificed.

~

~

Dennis Fitzpatrick and I danced cheek-to-cheek
on the last day of sixth grade.
Was my father's strained smile approval or reproach?

~

~

If I had become a boy I would be gay.
This vexes the brows in narrow pews:
given the choice even boys may choose boys.

IN LIEU OF FLOWERS

The apple tree broke into blossom the morning after the school dance.
The day before girls swarmed the boys' school campus, arriving
exotic as orchids to us, faculty brats who conferred to them
our bedrooms for the night. Their femininity—spritzes
of perfume and hairspray, sliding silks and taffetas,
whispers, laughter—so pervaded our house my father
couldn't stop chuckling to himself; my mother, the care-giver,
in the kitchen regretted something, frenching the beans and
searching drawers for the garlic press.

Oh those girls were marvelous and knew things about boys
that I, surrounded as I was by them, could only imagine.
There would be secrets and kissing and dancing close.
I spent that night on the chaise in my parents' room
and woke below window-framed apple blossoms,
the tree transformed overnight into a perfumed beauty
in a gown of pinks and white. As I would one day be?
The memory, my first miracle and swooning,
cleaves like Velcro—

That's why, if I did receive flowers, I would want not lilies
with their funereal odor, nor trite gladioli or even roses,
but clouds of apple blossoms with their promise of fruit
and the transfiguration of my small life.

REMEMBERED KISS

When she knows the chapel is empty she reaches the door's iron ring,
throws her weight against it, her bright heat spilling
into stone-vaulted air. Her eyes adjust to darkness
and sunlight through stained glass.
Crowds of griffins carved into rafters watch
as she savors this trespass, being a secret.
On bended knee, St. George shines in stillness. Her prayer:
let him collar her stalking beasts,
let her lead them to the meadow, nuzzle them.
They'll circle as she climbs into pines, blameless,
unreachable by whiskered cheek
or raised brow's impugning.
Sticky with pitch she pulls herself onto his knee,
kisses his marble lips until she,
wicked girl, is cooled and holy.

PHOTOGRAPH IN AN ALBUM

The bike, the kids, the man, the fact
that he is gone and everything dissolved.
Even the house destroyed. But she remembers
the day her father called them into the yard
to pose them for his parents.
She can feel the prick of spring grass on her thighs
and the sting of her imposture
as she spread her skirt around her princess-like,
radiating, she meant to, purity.
And the scratch of his wool shorts
as she gathered her brother into her lap.
Studying the photograph now it's not the dead
who move her but the Schwinn, remembering
the cards attached with a clothespin
that played her wheels' spokes, a bright staccato
echoing up the arcaded street where she could bike fastest
no hands, but wings, rapture of Kipling's jungle
beneath the apple trees in Pomfret, Connecticut.
What happened to her? Kidnapped? Hung from a hook
in the basement, next to Marcy and Anne? No
that was just her dream or premonition; the potent
happiness she harbored then was contraband
confiscated at the border when she escaped.

PORTENTS

Because your father's servants had more privileges than you
you couldn't wait to be rid of your childhood's enslavement.
To own yourself you had to flee. *I was freest then,*
floating in liquid days as effortlessly as on the lake
mottled with sunlight and leaf mold, tadpoles kissing
my shins. My grownups were unenviable, deprived
of nature's enchantments, uplift of wonderment.
Your 8-Ball (if you ever entertained its mundane
prophesy) answered all your wishes: *Not yet. Not yet.*
I smashed my 8-Ball on a rock disclosing its core:
a pyramid printed with predictions and prevarications
suspended in a jar of inky water.
My sources say no. Concentrate and ask again.
I hid my discovery in the stone wall by the bus stop.
It may be there still, murky vault of my future, turning
and ticking its tacit answers to questions I haven't asked.

ODE TO THE BODY

In the dark you unfold
irreproachably.
Alive.
How you lower yourself will be
your distinction: in pews, apology,
imploring. Gravity grabs you
by the shoulders,
perplexes you until
you are accustomed to its weight.
When *things start to happen:*
blood without wounds,
breasts, thrill
of his belt buckle
in the back of his uncle's
Mustang. Repulsed
by your thirst for him I
pretend not to know you.
Oh, the years
undressing, aching
to shed even your skin. I,
too afraid to follow you,
my offering,
into the damp
basement, the room
above the casino,
the wife's bedroom.

The pleasure yours
and all you had, the guilt
my just dessert. Exuberance.
You will have moments.
Olympian labors
of two pregnancies,
stone walls you'll build
and gardens. I will admire
the strength of your arms,
the pronounced veins
of your hands. I'll
resist a catalogue
of your diminishments.
Focus on the fire.
This second stage. You'll burn,
and not from yearning. Surges
of heat will rise from your
center to your scalp, melting
your wings. Unearthly
as some goddess as
you pass your prime.

PRODIGY

I grew up; a privilege not apportioned to my brothers,
one only an infant when
he took up canoodling with angels. Resenting me?
Bobby was younger but lasted
longer. At 30, disguised as a grownup, the hirsute cheek,
his body bristled
with lubricity, then malignancy
before he'd settled into life enough to look ahead.
He was the prodigy, but I
had genius enough for survival.

Taking fewer chances, I live on, accumulating
debt. Death is a hard act to follow. Who can compete?
Agnostics shed their angels. Forget that one. But
I want difficult Bobby back,
to look out to sea with him from my
weathered porch, both of us
dressed in tattered robes and lifting gin from doilies.

His grin usurps his face when he says—but I can't hear what he says;
only his laugh like coins dropping into a bowl.

DAVID

Handsome face framed by a halo of tight curls
he taught his cousins, my children, how to swim. He was
his sisters' mascot and treasure, mined.
Unsolved by college the problem of living
put him on a train with a map to his future.
Midnight. Ides of March. Bound for the beach, not
for romance, but sea as isolation's mirror.
Trussed by bonds that might have bound him
to us, our boy turned away, wild to be gone.
The night empties of all impulses save one.
Either there is no moon, no stars, or they are
in abundance. The cold has no consequence. Tides
don't mark the hour. Abraham's knife, pulled
from his pocket, doesn't glint, only murders.
No one speaks, stays or forces
his hand. Death is his chance, our lack.
This day's dawn won't conquer the dark.
We, relicts of his joy, wear black.

AT THE CEMETERY

The yellow backhoe idles near
meaning business.
We can't put down our shovels.
This is not a tucking in, but
pretends to be,
the story, the kiss, the lullaby.
Another shovelful of earth.
This ache in my shoulder's
a gift.
As long as I stall that
brute machine
I keep you ours, though
I could not keep you here.

PALUDAL

Praise the stench, layer upon layer of rot
and scum beneath a scrim of cum and lugworms' egg sacs
flung here and there. Step near
and be sucked down through strata of secretions,
black ooze, slick algae—meal of larval tongues.
Shitting, digging, feeding, purifying: silversides, gemma clams, winkles,
mummichogs. *What a congress of stinks!*
Life forms compose, decompose, all fecund and sunset smeared.
From their holes streams of fiddler crabs swarm and spit their balls of sand,
clacking like bones (or knitting needles).
Mud snails graze up and down the cordgrass with the tide. The night heron
abides.
Each essential to this varnished reek on which everything depends.

CONSIDER THE HORSESHOE CRAB

Actually, not a crab, but of the Chelicerata class with undersides
ruffled like pages and sword-like tails called telsons used, sometimes
successfully, to flip themselves over when they're wrong-side up.

There is hardly an obstacle they can overcome; yet they've witnessed
eons' passing, riding colliding continents in the Cenozoic era
long before we were a glimmer in god's eye.

Their springtime congresses, construed as battered helmets strewn
across a battlefield, speak instead of endurance, a magisterial longevity
that trenches and tanks don't signify.

Vulnerable as prank fodder, eel bait, and pharmacological commodity—
their blue blood used to signal traces of bacteria—these ancients might
one day supply detection of life forms in outermost space.

In the here and now they make untroubled progress over the sands
and keep their secrets.

I imagine such a history for myself, such purposeful
plodding over this benevolent, unsympathetic earth.

INTO MY GARDEN

The bees are pulsing on the thyme
entering shafts of digitalis blooms
as if they were rooms at a Motel 6.
Slippity-slap their black rumps quake,
prick the swollen stigma.
Insensible, stock-still stalks depend
on bees for conversation and lovemaking.
Where's the hive where the queen wakes
with craving, majuscule amid pews of six-sided cells,
where she pierces her drowsy sisters with poison,
sucks royal jelly from her nurses' heads,
and is drawn to the portal between the dark
and her imperative?
She pauses there, trembles, then soars.
launching herself in nuptial flight to such a height
only a few drones will reach her.
In flight they'll entwine
in brainless ecstasy until the males are emptied,
dismembered, seared husks
plummeting invisibly to rest
amid all this growing stuff.

WEEDING IN WELLFLEET

Beyond lies the sea, an open drawer of knives catching light.
The blade of my hoe eats as a goat eats at roots of self-seeding
arugula, clover, and blame. Praise all things that thrive without
intervention. All alimentation and upkeep insists on murder.

I chose the garden as I chose love. Could have left well-enough
alone, let the sands drift to the edge of the patio, beggared
of my shovelfuls of manure and peat now nurturing phlox,
lady's mantle, delphinium, rudbeckia, monarda, rose,

cascades of color giving suck to long-tongued butterflies and bees.
I might have lingered in the shade of encroaching pines observing
the snails' slime trails, the black streak of voles, the cruel-eyed crow,
without the postulate to protect what I've come to call mine.

BACKYARD CONDOTTIERI

I invited beauty into the yard,
scooped out a pond, planted water lilies.
The great blue heron came and dipped his bill,
then frogs, snakes, even larger frogs, to feed
on each other. Who knew a frog would eat
a bird? I lured orioles with oranges,
welcomed the shock of bluebirds whose color
was quarried from the lapis lazuli Giotto
would need for that sky behind St. Francis.
Sweet, sweet, sweet's the cardinal's song, ruined
by garrulous grackles and hooded cowbirds
that lay their eggs in others' nests.
On this parade's periphery, erect,
the robin distinguishes her enterprise
from grackles' grab at what's not freely given.
Finally twilight.
The mercenaries quit their quest,
clatter off to the west, scattering their loot
across the hillside.
The princely cardinal
enters the square, irresistible as prayer,
an instant's stillness everywhere.

THE TWENTY-NINTH BATHER

You splash in the water there, yet stay stock still in your room.
  "Song of Myself [11]"

You walk the tide's edge,
footfall, wave lick, glint,
the bay's light-stitched pleats
suddenly ripped by frenzy
as if a serpent
aroused by hunger seethed
through weedy seas to this shore,
now scissoring the air with snapping teeth,
tails flashing.
Undress for your lover,
seize and be seized:
let the wild water rise
from ankles to thighs,
dive through its welted surface,
plough the waves with your yearning.

MIGRAINE ON THE AEGEAN

While gazing at ruins we met a goat
with drooped grey ears and a black and white coat.
He had the face of a philosopher
and black eyes that were lensed with gossamer.

His indifference to history was complete:
the arch above him, rubble at his feet,
even Praxiteles' Aphrodite
could not intrude, move him to piety.

Now I'm below decks, sulking and in pain,
craving the dark of my berth. It's a shame
when about me all the elements shine
this ransacked utopia—almost mine.

Now listening I hear persistent bleats.
That goat and I are bound by our conceits.

THIS COMPOST

It has a fulsome fetor. Leavings from feasts rich with fruit, pungent
with mold, leguminous slops mixed into dregs, dross, and dung where
worms like cuticle parings writhe in the mix and leaven it for its purpose
as pabulum, sub rosa, in the garden. Nothing like the garbaged fish head
alive with maggots that fills the yard with the stench of battlefield, this stuff
is all perfumed potential. Not dust to dust, but cabbage to cabbage, coffee
grounds to rose. What chemistry! Am I not a mahatma as I turn my barrel
into provender for turnips?

SUMMER NIGHT

Speak-speak / speak-speak /
so say the crickets.
The cicadas' pitched hum
spins a blade.
They're troubled, but lack thumbs
or whatever distinguishes us.
Thumbs and music making;
though, as for music, they're trying:
hear us who remind you of summer nights
and boys who forgot themselves
in wanting to know
the feel of anyone else's flesh. Desperate.
We are so desperate for radiance, melody, or
from another continent, a breeze
that doesn't reek of ashes.

THE DOWSERS

The orphaned and misshapen, our school's gift from the local
       foster home, had divining rods for wells of kindness,

a sixth sense: Sharon Getty disappeared her irises during fire drills,
       locked me to her then peed herself and my sneakers;
I made up a story that she'd lost her family in a fire;
       misconstrued Pat Scull had much wrong with her and me as friend;
John Payne was speech impeded, but passed love notes from his desk to mine;
       all were drawn to me.

My father watching westerns punched the air during fistfights,
       faked and dodged on the couch when Saturday games were on.
Turns out a surfeit of mirror neurons wired us for empathy.
       His spectating brain spoke directly to his muscle, mine
lost my home to fire, lost my perfect body to some mischance.

I was connected to every living thing and might have been a Jain
       if I'd known there were alternatives to Jesus
for whose crucifixion I was sorry, sorry, sorry.

My father dedicated himself to civil rights through the sixties
       but retreated to his island when he could, to feel
the benefit of his luck without reproach.

There are those with a deficit of mirror neurons. Must be.

See the teenaged soldiers posing on the flatbed truck holding their AK-47s the way teenaged mothers hold their babies.

NOTHING GOOD CAN COME OF THIS

I never got the tits predicted in the magazines
or the length of leg I must have conceived.
I flunked *love and work* as Freud would have it.
On choosing love I grew distracted.

I failed to rescue two brothers and a nephew—
though I am pretty sure I didn't kill them—
and never could reassure Mother or make her
happy, though I could make her laugh.

My life is unpublished, another's unwritten.
My failures—oh, they are legion—form the canal
I stumble into whenever a funk overtakes me,
each lock releasing me into higher humiliation.

Now, everything—except the belittlements—I forget:
my glasses in the diner, purse on the park bench,
my umbrella in the dojo.

IS THIS WHAT YOU EXPECTED?

That I can't change purses with lady-like authority?
That I will never be the committee co-chair photographed
with the author she's reeled in like a marlin, or the first
woman CEO of the all-male bastion (like a river
against a root ambition—I've willed myself
against it—streams in me).
That I shrink from praise yet feel the blame of parenthood;
that approaching the make-up counter at Bergdorf's,
I will hope the blushed and burnished woman
wielding her sponges and paints will make me over
from inside out. I burn with regret and a longing to do
the whole thing over again, to have another chance,
to win you on some other terms.

SECRET MISBEHAVIOR

Being inclines intrinsically to self-concealment.
Mother standing beside the basement freezer
in the dark with a gallon of chocolate ice cream
and a spoon, the lies we tell to normalize or dramatize;

our secrets' shroud disguises us from the world
or from our guilt, bestows a flavor we learn to crave;
sheathed in silk, the razor-scarred arm, the bottle drawn
not casually from a cupboard, cigarette out the window,

draughts of poisons drawn deep into selves flabbergasted by dullness.

Heraclitus: fragment 123

DAWN

Mother Fakes Daughter's Cancer for Cash
Dateline: Urbana, Ohio

My life? It's like I'm stalled at the intersection's stop sign
and all the other cars move forward except for mine.
What I needed was a hardship I could advertise,
a cause to make the neighbors sympathize.

So, I glued Dawn's bruised face to collecting cans,
to telephone poles, a few delivery vans.
My disrespectful daughter now a wounded sparrow
and me—I went from lowlife to local hero.

Hearing the cancer was faked they want their money back,
have forced me to return the goddam Cadillac.
Rancor streams from church groups, the Elks, the Grange.
Still I'm stalled at that stop sign. My life won't change.

WITHHOLDING

The injection of pentobarbital instantly morphed our dog into a fur
sack of bones: *where does the wag go?* Perhaps an energy exchange
occurs, a transformation, as happens with metaphor.

My mother's eyes turn bluer and recognize no one.
She no longer stirs, knits, strokes my arm, or waves *hello.*
Pinned to dimness she seems a citizen from a fractured world,

resting her un-capable hand on mine. I would call her
soulless, but, she can't give it up and until she does
she cannot enter mine.

FAMILY PLOT

Three portraits hang above our mother's bed, have done
from house to house to house to home. These are the faces
of her children at three years old, two formal portraits and one
a candid shot of me, middle child placed on the right
in my mother's scheme: instead of chronologically, a hostess's
girl-boy seating plan with baby Bobby in the middle, central,
the hoped-for solution to her puzzled haplessness.

Her literal composition had always amused, as if
our faces were pressed flowers stemming upwards
from the fertile ground of her marriage bed. Today I study
the lovely roundness of my sister's curls, her cheeks,
her before-all-this innocence in sepia tones. Bobby's face
actually glows: eyes shining with amusement, a puckish
mischievousness, the cause of his death in its benign phase.

THE SEAMSTRESS

My mother never forgave my father his outside interests.
Is that true? He was the only one she, practitioner of denial,
didn't blame, grateful to him for her escape from a father
prone to violence, and the cramped mundane she was heir to.

Regarding my lacerated fingertip—encounter with a wood chipper—
I think how like him I am in my reckless competence. My work shed holds
chainsaws, staple guns, toggle bolts, drills, but no calendar with Miss July
showing her tits. No sewing machine.

My mother could never forgive my father his defense of me,
or so he must have thought, since he never dissuaded her,
whose very optic nerve aligned itself against me,
or assuaged her jealousy of my easy childhood.

They were best left alone, prom queen and prom king, without
suggestion that their days were fraught with insufficiencies,
without the word-shit flying from my untamable mouth,
without a reminder that even care can stir up intractable currents.

Still, she sleeps with his framed photograph on the pillow
while we, the living, re-stitch the seams of love that she,
not liking the fit, had so intently picked apart in her better days.
My mother could never forgive my father his dying.

HER VOICE

New to walking and never far,
I am climbing the concrete steps
next to the gymnasium
on the school grounds
beside my mother
when I fall.

She speaks my name with alarm
as if,
waking from a dream,
she is surprised by my presence,
as if
both of us,
suddenly,
were real.

All these years later—
often as I'm on the brink of sleep—
her voice drops
into my hearing
like nectar
naming me.

GRATIFIED DESIRE

If you lifted the "house" from "housewife"
it would not be such a bad job,
not partnered to rooms or dust,
but to the man,
the small burden of laughing
at repeated jokes.
Who wouldn't admire
the woman's shining competence at love
and accommodation?
the lineaments of practiced ardor?
Yes, there's abnegation,
but wife burns.
Enough to set the house on fire.

AZOIC

She began her dictionary project in her final month,
composing sentences with the words she'd found:
The angiography revealed no angioma.
At ataxia she felt her first contraction and ceded control.

So many hours later she reclaimed her body to push-relax-push,
the opposite of reeling in a fish. On the outpouring rush of fluid:
water, blood, piss, more water, out flowed her Moses. But, what is this?
A furball coated with vernix and lanugo wails. She wails, too.

So ceases her ataraxia—from the Greek ataraktos—
the state of being undisturbed.

OUR FOUR-YEAR-OLD SON LEARNS OF DEATH

The brat next door has told you all of us will die.
I'm unprepared.
Want to shout: Not so! Never me. Not you.
You're full of tears.
Both of us wounded by the news
and I, unwilling to describe a paradise
you'd have to die to know.

Come to the window.
See the starlight dancing on the snowy field?

If you were dying I would make you a heaven
your friends would envy. But I won't
dazzle you with angels who might lift you
out of fear. Away from me.
That brat abused your tenderness, but didn't lie.
Death is true
as the rush of the pasture stream in springtime
weaving gold through the field.

There's heaven for you, where
any god you want is yours.
Choose one who will bend you
in reverence not remorse.

TO A TERRAPIN

Mid-June I begin listening for you—
telltale rustling in the understory
as you make your way
through deadfall
and I welcome your approach,
admire your shell,
medallion of polygon tesserae,
an elephant's saggy ankles, your flesh,
smooth and warm as scrotum.
Is this what snakes feel like?
I'll never know.
You have no reverse
in motion or thought as you,
single-minded,
shamble from the marsh's muck
to this patch of compacted sand,
indifferent
to the abiding appetites
of fox and snake,
and dig and dig with clawed paws
swift and agile as a croupier's hands,
deposit your eggs
then cover and tamp
and have the job of mothering not begun,
but done.
The skunk takes note.

HUMMINGBIRDS

They hover like funambulists without a rope, these smallest
in the order Apodiformes. As the begonia has no scent, they have no song,
but the trill of their wings, and a screak when alarmed.
It's the S/inverse S motion of their wings that allows them to fly
in place and in reverse and all the way here from Mexico.

Heat until dissolved:
one part sugar to four parts water. Your brew
will have the aroma of a nidus in a peach and be as fine
as any acanthus offers up to their grooved tongues.
Watch as their ruby gorgets thrum with swallows—sip, sip,
sip, as from the lily's lip.

One dusk, come fall, they'll suck their fill then depart
for the Yucatan, fueled by your concoction. They'll hover
near Calakmul's Mayan pyramid, dipping bills into
passion flowers without a single thought of you.

AFTER ICE, EVERYTHING ELSE

Because I've drowned the phantom sharks and real leeches,
accept that snakes slide beneath me,
and that the snapping turtle earns his place,
I can share with my daughter my knack for floating.
Once a piece of ice, shaped as this pond is, broke away,
its borders shored by the glacier's relinquished debris as it ebbed.
Honeysuckle grows here now, pines, scrub oak, whatever took
after forests were axed to build Boston.
We drift on our backs our arms outstretched, hands
cupped by water, palms cupping the sky. The water
responds to our breathing, lifts us then pulls us back.
To the east the ocean proclaims and surrenders.

AGRIGENTO

In the Valley of Temples, high on a cliff by the sea without oarsmen
Helios sets sandstone aflame in his arc over columns
lifting a darkening sky.
My girl's cheek, too, is golden, flawless.
Cross-legged on the altar, we imagine white heifer,
bloodied gash, entrails for prophesy, incantations
for the unsettled bride. Fierce Hera,
ox-eyed goddess, pacified, while horned Io stumbles
on hooves once flesh. Exile, gift of her father's faith in oracles,
maddening gadfly, the price of jealousy.
Belief builds monuments and plunders them.
Lydia is bride to doubt.
These toppled thrones provoke us to blandness.
Why not invent a god for every occasion?
Don deities like new dresses. Summon whichever gods
survived the pillaging, the years:
Let the muses sing. Let us not be too dull to hear.

APOLOGY TO MY SON

You confided in me your 12-year-old sorrow
saying: "No one I know feels like this."

I might have tongued it away like a mother cat.
Instead, afraid an auscultation of your heart would show
my own disorder passed on to you,
I said: "I'll get your father."

I'm relieved that you didn't swallow the poison
like some king's taster, but spoke instead.
We are solitary beings and at times it feels unbearable.
Some are better at assuming masks of happy selves.

I might have said: happy or sad you are necessary, beloved, my own.
Wed your loneliness and one day wed another's.

WHAT SORT OF GRANDMOTHER

when water and sky are swollen, gunmetal grey
and the egret wading in the marsh is a white that makes
everything else in the world recede, and the slightest
motion of oar, trailing hand, or leaf creates a wake
that might circle the globe and return to lap
this particular silence as heat transforms
to needle the sky with lightning, and day
plays starless night,
takes the child,
yes, with a lifejacket, in the kayak
and shows her the wild peace of the world?
and who's to say which is fossil
and which is living creature leaving its mark?

.

SLACK TIDE

The interval begins as Earth reaches behind her back
to loosen her straps for this easy span of fullness.
The ocean briefly ceases its slap and chisel against our shore.

Calm curls around clashings
and the gathering ghosts of squandered sons
who pulsed into life and will not grow old:

now yearbook picture shrines in shuttered living rooms,
now apparitions in sea foam, elegiac shadows and suspended light.
Pounded by sorrow we apply the bandage of valor to calamity.

But within this tidal moment, as loud with silence as an empty music hall,
there is no assault and no resistance. On Manhattan, when the Hudson's
currents slow to ironed seams, even city traffic glides into stillness.

Far inland a mother presses her forehead against cool glass. Out on the sea
my kayak rises on the swell, buoyed between intractable continents.
All is becalmed in a suspension of time before the tide's turning.

The world's abyssal intake of breath, then lamentation.

THEN

The day was gorgeous, everyone said so,
the sky a shellacked, pupil-piercing blue
when it was riven by two planes, two pilots
who had learned to fly but not land.
The interruption might have been as ravishing
as the murmuration of starlings—the pulsing
crescendo and diminuendo that startles the air
when on their periphery a falcon is sensed;
their flight not choreographed by a commander,
but folkmind, a collective synchrony as if
neurotransmitters fired from a single gland.

Didn't some of us—before that day—wish
sometimes for something to fall from the sky
and enliven things? As there are those who
love the wild smell of hurricane winds
and the charged arousal of the ocean until/
unless their forfeit is too great.

On this day unwinged beings took to the sky.
There was nothing left for the coroners.

THE DARLING BOY

i

If you hide in the linen closet
I will find you;
only the house is gone.
You were never at home
in your body, as if you'd been
given the wrong size: face
too loose, shoulders too tight,
arms too long. Were you ever
convinced it was yours?
I prayed you'd come: a blaze
of happiness undoing the curse,
infant prince in the glass coffin.

ii

Our first time together in New Orleans. (Too late.
You're ashes.) Your boyfriend George drives us
to Galatoire's in his '78 Caddy. Passing a diner
George points: *There's a place we went for breakfast*
almost every day. Come to think of it, for a Jew,
(A Jew?) *Bobby sure could eat a lot of bacon!*
The blood stops moving through my veins.
Our Protestant parents occupy the silence
of the back seat, hands folded in their laps.

Our avoidance is instinctive as a bat's.
It's too late to wake the dreamers.
If I speak I could, like you, ruin everything.

iii
You are ridden by your body's imperatives
to New Orleans where you can drink gin at dawn,
dress as Hitler for Mardi Gras. *But, he's Jewish
and gay*, your friends say to deter angry revelers.
A maddening bartender, when the customer asks
for change you light a match to his fifty.
Tolerance is love's sick cousin: why not have fun?
So real your inheritance of horror that when
AIDS ignites your body you believe you're dying
in the camps, your life—carnival without Lent,
abandon without repose, most real when you were
dying and when you were born again, giving
yourself a second chance at being loved.
None of us, not even you, managed that.
Your genius: tailoring a wound for each of us
out of the bloodied garments of your own.

iv
We sit halfway up the stairs holding
hands, a flimsy life raft in a storm
of slamming doors and objects thrown.

She's unhappy, I say. You're confused:
a father who laughs when he's angry,
a mother who rages when sad, a sister
who won't say: *This stinks*. Still, you find
the center to spin out from and away.
(Last year, from a newspaperman you knew
in college: *God, he was handsome! And so
charismatic!* Could you have known that?
Enough for me to be happy for days.)

v

We're drawn by slow horses—how bright the day!
—behind Duke Dejan's brass band, searching
the second-line marchers for faces we'll recognize,
even understand: the bar-owner in his mother's
leopard-skin pillbox, parade of your comrades
wearied from camp or combat. My missing brother.
"Flee as a Bird" rises to high windowsills,
finds its way beyond iron-lace fences.
A bantam boy prances the sidelines, taps, fills
the gaps that mourning steals from cadences.
Our sorrow floods the street and laps the curb
where unremarkable life continues undisturbed.

vi

Our parade ends at your bar.
The family that's misplaced you
as incongruous here as you
in their West Hartford. Our father,
too, a master of disguise in white suit,
white-brimmed hat, red suspenders.
Around us all the talk's of you, a fable
—innuendo or exact, high jinx and turning
tricks—the more explicit the more impossibly
abstract (Mom even found a woman to praise
your performance as Eeyore). Only
three bourbons 'til Dad chuckles
You know, I sort of envy him this life.
Did he pass the wish on to you
like a note under the table?

vii

I lift you out of the tub.
Still slippery with soap you flee
my arms, run from the house
into the field, naked and shimmering.
If you'd only kept running.
Any other family. Any other life.

IF ONLY NATURE

Green to the very door! (as Wordsworth wrote) has been my ambition.
If only nature would mind.
This explains my vehemence against the copulating beetles on the roses
performing all functions at once,
the voles who chewed the roots of the viburnums (fifty dollars each)
killing them in their winter sleep,
the starlings aswarm at the feeder while the smaller birds take to the trees,
the squirrels who gnawed through the shed's door to homestead there
(snakes are merely surprising),
the mediocre poet whose self-promotion has been rewarded.
Freud boils motive down to money and sex. Maybe it's ownership.
All transactions come with expectations:
the fragrant blooms from shrubbery, morning's calls for more bird seed.
I want the fox, the turtle, the owl,
but not the snail hiding its slime inside a yellow helix
as it poisons the monkshood.
To taste the fruit of my labors I preserve it from slugs and thieves,
but, in truth, I envy them their disregard and greed.

Acknowledgments

Certain of these poems are dedicated in memorium:
"August," to my father, Robert A. Lazear
"Portents," to Ben Sonnenberg
"David," to my nephew, David Okrent
"The Darling Boy," to my brother, Bobby Lazear

"The Seamstress" owes a debt to Stanley Kunitz's poem, "The Portrait."

Thanks to the editors who published poems in earlier versions and offered encouragement:

Richard Howard for *Western Humanities Review*; Henri Cole for *The New Republic*; John Skoyles for *Ploughshares*; and Patricia Carlin for *Barrow Street*.

Other poems have appeared in *New Millennium Writings, Provincetown Arts, Morning Song:Poems for New Parents*, published by St. Martin's Press, and *World of Water World of Sand: A Cape Cod Collection of Poetry, Fiction and Memoir*.

Lynn Emanuel gave the manuscript an early and helpful reading.

I am grateful to Dana Prescott and the Civitella Ranieri Foundation for the gift of unfettered weeks in Umbria in the company of spirited fellows and all those Giottos and Pieros.

Thanks to Martha Rhodes for her friendship and sage counsel, and for giving my poems and others' a life between covers. I tip my hat to Ryan Murphy and all the Four Way Books staff.

For many years Provincetown's Fine Arts Work Center has provided time and space to artists of varied disciplines. There I've had the pleasure of working with a number of dedicated poets, both emerging and in full leaf. Of those, I am particularly indebted to Henri Cole and Marie Ponsot.

I am lucky in friends and family whose thoughtful kindness sustains me. Dan makes all things possible.

Rebecca Okrent's prose has appeared in various publications including *The Boston Globe*, *The New York Times Magazine* and *Book Review*, and *Travel & Leisure*. Journals in which her poems have appeared include *Barrow Street*, *The New Republic*, *Ploughshares*, and *Western Humanities Review*. She and her husband, the writer Daniel Okrent, divide their time between Manhattan and Cape Cod. This is her first book.